For Patrick

With thanks to Selina Hastings,
who made the initial selection of rhymes.

Introduction by David Lloyd.

First published 1985 by Walker Books Ltd
184-192 Drummond Street London NW1 3HP

Illustrations © 1985 Charlotte Voake

First printed 1985
Printed and bound in Italy by L.E.G.O., Vicenza.

British Library Cataloguing in Publication Data
Over the moon: a book of nursery rhymes.
1. Nursery rhymes, English
I. Voake, Charlotte
398'.8   PZ8.1

ISBN 0-7445-0337-X

OVER THE
MOON

A Book of
NURSERY RHYMES

Index of First Lines, Pages 118-121

Illustrated by
Charlotte Voake

WALKER BOOKS
LONDON

It is unheard of that a cow should jump over the moon anywhere except in the world of nursery rhymes. But it only needs someone to speak the words hey diddle diddle, or hickory dickory dock, or rub-a-dub-dub, and anything can happen.

The world described by the rhymes in this book is wild, gentle, happy, sad, crazy, sensible and always filled with extraordinary delight. Each generation passes on this delight to the next at the earliest possible opportunity.

Nursery rhymes come new and fresh to every child, but many of them are very old. 'Hey Diddle Diddle' first appeared in print more than two hundred years ago, and it was probably an old rhyme even then.

Many of the rhymes were never originally intended for children — they may be parts of old songs or adult jokes, or all that remains of ancient customs and traditions. Scholars have spent years researching their true meaning — claiming that 'Mary, Mary, Quite Contrary' is really about Mary, Queen of Scots; 'Ring-a-ring o' Roses' was an invocation against the plague; or 'Jack and Jill' derives from a Scandinavian moon myth. None of this matters to children. They take the rhymes at their face value and love the sound of the words without worrying about their sense.

Open this book anywhere and you see the essential images of childhood. The objects, the animals, the curious characters, the vivid scenes — they belong to children and the child in everyone. Charlotte Voake's wonderful illustrations are filled with the same jubilant spirit as the rhymes. They are an invitation to all children to be happy come what may — as happy as that unique, fantastically athletic cow.

A B C D E F G H I J K L M N O P Q R S T U V W X Y Z

E eat it

C cut it

B bit it

F fought for it

D dealt it

A was an apple pie

XYZ and & all
wished for a piece
in hand

W wanted it

V viewed it

U upset it

G got it

I inspected it

J joined for it

H had it

K kept it

L longed for it

M mourned for it

N nodded at it

O opened it

P peeped in it

Q quartered it

S stole it

R ran for it

T took it

Z Y X W V U T S R Q P O N M L K J I H G F E D C B A

ABCDEFGHIJKLMNOPQRSTUVWXYZ

Georgie Porgie, pudding and pie,
Kissed the girls and made them cry.
When the boys came out to play,
Georgie Porgie ran away.

Lucy Locket lost her pocket,
Kitty Fisher found it.
Not a penny was there in it,
Only ribbon round it.

On Saturday night I lost my wife,
  And where do you think I found her?
Up in the moon, singing a tune,
  And all the stars around her.

Sally go round the sun,
  Sally go round the moon,
Sally go round the chimney-pots
  On a Saturday afternoon.

There was an old woman who lived in a shoe,
She had so many children she didn't know what to do.
She gave them some broth without any bread.
She whipped them all soundly and put them to bed.

Hey diddle, diddle,
The cat and the fiddle,
    The cow jumped over the moon.
The little dog laughed
To see such sport,
    And the dish ran away with the spoon.

The man in the moon
    Came tumbling down,
        And asked his way to Norwich.
He went by the south,
And burnt his mouth
        With supping cold pease-porridge.

Jerry Hall,
He is so small,
A rat could eat him,
Hat and all.

Six little mice sat down to spin.
Pussy passed by and she peeped in.
What are you doing, my little men?
Weaving coats for gentlemen.
Shall I come in and cut off your threads?
No, no, Mistress Pussy, you'd bite off our heads.
Oh, no, I'll not; I'll help you to spin.
That may be so, but you don't come in.

Pussy cat, pussy cat,
　Where have you been?
I've been to London
　To look at the Queen.
Pussy cat, pussy cat,
　What did you there?
I frightened a little mouse
　Under her chair.

Pretty maid, pretty maid,
　Where have you been?
Gathering roses
　To give to the Queen.
Pretty maid, pretty maid,
　What gave she you?
She gave me a diamond,
　As big as my shoe.

Little Bo-Peep has lost her sheep,
 And doesn't know where to find them.
Leave them alone, and they'll come home
 Bringing their tails behind them.

Little Bo-Peep fell fast asleep,
 And dreamt she heard them bleating.
But when she awoke, she found it a joke,
 For they were still a-fleeting.

Then up she took her little crook,
    Determined for to find them.
She found them indeed, but it made her heart bleed,
    For they'd left all their tails behind them.

It happened one day as Bo-Peep did stray
    Into a meadow hard by,
There she espied their tails side by side,
    All hung on a tree to dry.

She heaved a sigh and wiped her eye,
    Then went o'er hill and dale,
And tried what she could, as a shepherdess should,
    To tack to each sheep its tail.

Three young rats with black felt hats,
Three young ducks with white straw flats,
Three young dogs with curling tails,
Three young cats with demi-veils,
Went out to walk with two young pigs
In satin vests and sorrel wigs.
But suddenly it chanced to rain
And so they all went home again.

Hoddley, poddley,
Puddle and fogs,
Cats are to marry
The poodle dogs.
Cats in blue jackets
And dogs in red hats,
What will become
Of the mice and the rats?

There was a rat, for want of stairs,
Went down a rope to say his prayers.

There was a crooked man,
  And he walked a crooked mile,

He found a crooked sixpence
  Against a crooked stile.

How many miles to Babylon?
  Threescore miles and ten.
Can I get there by candle-light?
  Yes, and back again.
If your heels are nimble and light,
  You may get there by candle-light.

There was a jolly miller once,
    Lived on the river Dee.
He worked and sang from morn till night,
    No lark more blithe than he.
And this the burden of his song
    Forever used to be,
I care for nobody, no! not I,
    If nobody cares for me.

He bought a crooked cat,
    Which caught a crooked mouse,

And they all lived together
In a little crooked house.

Tuesday's child
is full of grace

Monday's child is
fair of face

Friday's child is
loving and giving

Saturday's child
works hard for a living

Wednesday's
child is full of woe

Thursday's child
Has far to go

And the child that
is born on the
Sabbath Day
Is bonny and blithe, and good and gay.

Solomon Grundy,
Born on a Monday,

Christened on Tuesday,

Married on Wednesday,

Took ill on Thursday,

Worse on Friday,

Died on Saturday,

Buried on Sunday.

This is the end
Of Solomon Grundy.

Hark, hark,
The dogs do bark,
    The beggars are coming to town;
Some in rags,
And some in jags,
    And one in a velvet gown.

Rub-a-dub-dub,
Three men in a tub,
    And how do you think they got there?
The butcher, the baker,
The candlestick-maker,
They all jumped out of a rotten potato,
    'Twas enough to make a man stare.

My mother said
I never should
Play with the gipsies
In the wood.
If I did she would say,
Naughty girl to disobey.
Your hair shan't curl,
Your shoes shan't shine,
You naughty girl,
You shan't be mine.
My father said
That if I did
He'd bang my head
With the teapot lid.

The wood was dark
The grass was green,
Up comes Sally
With a tambourine.
Alpaca frock,
New scarf-shawl,
White straw bonnet
And a pink parasol.
I went to the river
No ship to get across,
I paid ten shillings
For an old blind horse.
I up on his back
And off in a crack,
Sally, tell my mother
I shall never come back.

Four stiff-standers,
Four dilly-danders,
Two lookers,
Two crookers,
And a wig-wag.

Black I am and much admired,
Men seek for me until they're tired;
When they find me, break my head,
And take me from my resting bed.

Thirty white horses
Upon a red hill,
Now they stamp,
Now they champ,
Now they stand still.

Little Nancy Etticoat,
With a white petticoat,
And a red nose.
She has no feet or hands,
The longer she stands
The shorter she grows.

In spring I look gay,
Decked in comely array,
 In summer more clothing I wear;
When colder it grows,
I fling off my clothes,
 And in winter quite naked appear.

In marble walls as white as milk,
Lined with a skin as soft as silk,
Within a fountain crystal-clear,
A golden apple doth appear.
No doors there are to this stronghold,
Yet thieves break in and steal the gold.

Old Mother Twitchett has but one eye,
And a long tail which she can let fly,
And every time she goes over a gap,
She leaves a bit of her tail in a trap.

If all the world were paper,
  And all the sea were ink,
If all the trees were bread and cheese,
  What should we have to drink?

It's enough to make a man like me
  Scratch his head and think.

The man in the wilderness asked me,
How many strawberries grow in the sea?
I answered him, as I thought good,
As many as red herrings grow in the wood.

To market, to market,
To buy a fat pig,
Home again, home again,
Jiggety-jig.
To market, to market,
To buy a fat hog,
Home again, home again,
Jiggety-jog.

Barber, barber, shave a pig,
How many hairs will make a wig?
Four-and-twenty, that's enough,
Give the barber a pinch of snuff.

Elsie Marley is grown so fine,
She won't get up to feed the swine,
But lies in bed till eight or nine.
    Lazy Elsie Marley.

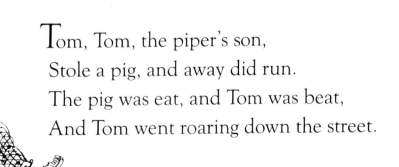

Tom, Tom, the piper's son,
Stole a pig, and away did run.
The pig was eat, and Tom was beat,
And Tom went roaring down the street.

Jack and Jill went up the hill
To fetch a pail of water.
Jack fell down and broke his crown,
And Jill came tumbling after.

Then up Jack got and home did trot
As fast as he could caper.
And went to bed to mend his head
With vinegar and brown paper.

33

Sukey, you shall be my wife
    And I will tell you why.
I have got a little pig,
    And you have got a sty.
I have got a dun cow,
    And you can make good cheese.
Sukey, will you marry me?
    Say Yes, if you please.

Curly locks, curly locks,
  Wilt thou be mine?
Thou shalt not wash dishes
  Nor yet feed the swine.
But sit on a cushion
  And sew a fine seam,
And feed upon strawberries,
  Sugar and cream.

Polly put the kettle on,
Polly put the kettle on,
Polly put the kettle on,
    We'll all have tea.

Sukey take it off again,
Sukey take it off again,
Sukey take it off again,
    They're all gone away.

Pat-a-cake, pat-a-cake, baker's man,
Bake me a cake as fast as you can.
Pat it and prick it, and mark it with T,
Put it in the oven for Tommy and me.

Cross-patch,
Draw the latch,
  Sit by the fire and spin;
Take a cup,
And drink it up,
  Then call your neighbours in.

Little Polly Flinders
Sat among the cinders
  Warming her pretty little toes.
Her mother came and caught her,
And whipped her little daughter
  For spoiling her nice new clothes.

There was a little girl, and she had a little curl
   Right in the middle of her forehead.
When she was good she was very, very good,
   But when she was bad she was horrid.

One day she went upstairs, while her parents, unawares,
   In the kitchen were occupied with meals.
And she stood upon her head, on her little truckle-bed,
   And then began hurraying with her heels.

Her mother heard the noise and thought it was the boys,
   A-kicking up a rumpus in the attic.
But when she climbed the stair, and saw Jemima there,
   She took her and did whip her most emphatic.

Girls and boys, come out to play,
The moon doth shine as bright as day.
Leave your supper, and leave your sleep,
And come with your playfellows into the street.
Come with a whoop, come with a call,
Come with a good will or not at all.
Up the ladder and down the wall,
A halfpenny roll will serve us all.
You find milk and I'll find flour,
And we'll have a pudding in half an hour.

Ring-a-ring o' roses,
A pocket full of posies,
A-tishoo! A-tishoo!
    We all fall down.

The cows are in the meadow
Lying fast asleep,
A-tishoo! A-tishoo!
    We all get up again.

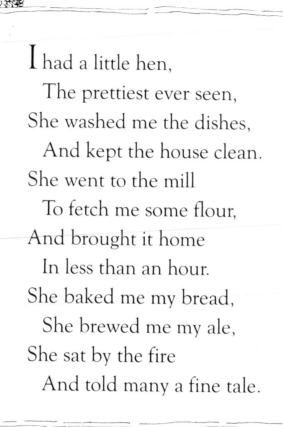

I had a little hen,
　　The prettiest ever seen,
She washed me the dishes,
　　And kept the house clean.
She went to the mill
　　To fetch me some flour,
And brought it home
　　In less than an hour.
She baked me my bread,
　　She brewed me my ale,
She sat by the fire
　　And told many a fine tale.

Hickety, pickety, my black hen,
She lays eggs for gentlemen.
Gentlemen come every day
To see what my black hen doth lay.

A farmer went trotting upon his grey mare,
  Bumpety, bumpety, bump!
With his daughter behind him so rosy and fair,
  Lumpety, lumpety, lump!

A raven cried, Croak! and they all tumbled down,
  Bumpety, bumpety, bump!
The mare broke her knees and the farmer his crown,
  Lumpety, lumpety, lump!

The mischievous raven flew laughing away,
  Bumpety, bumpety, bump!
And vowed he would serve them the same the next day,
  Lumpety, lumpety, lump!

I had a little pony,
His name was Dapple Gray.

I lent him to a lady
To ride a mile away.
She whipped him, she slashed him,
She rode him through the mire.

I would not lend my pony now,
For all the lady's hire.

Little Miss Muffet
Sat on a tuffet,
   Eating her curds and whey.
Along came a spider,
And sat down beside her
   And frightened Miss Muffet away.

Incey Wincey Spider
Climbed the water spout.
Down came the rain
And washed poor Wincey out.

Out came the sun
And dried up all the rain,
So Incey Wincey Spider
Climbed the spout again.

I had a little nut tree,
　Nothing would it bear
But a silver nutmeg
　And a golden pear.
The king of Spain's daughter
　Came to visit me,
And all for the sake
　Of my little nut tree.
I skipped over water,
　I danced over sea,
And all the birds in the air
　Couldn't catch me.

Mary, Mary, quite contrary,
How does your garden grow?
With silver bells and cockle shells,
And pretty maids all in a row.

Baa, baa, black sheep,
Have you any wool?
Yes, sir, yes, sir,
Three bags full;

One for the master,

And one for the dame,

And one for the little boy
Who lives down the lane.

Mary had a little lamb,
  Its fleece was white as snow.
And everywhere that Mary went
  The lamb was sure to go.

It followed her to school one day,
  Which was against the rule.
It made the children laugh and play
  To see a lamb at school.

I know a funny little man,
As quiet as a mouse,
Who does the mischief that is done
In everybody's house.
There's no one ever sees his face,
And yet we all agree
That every plate we break was cracked
By Mr Nobody.

'Tis he who always tears our books,
Who leaves the door ajar,
He pulls the buttons from our shirts,
And scatters pins afar.
That squeaking door will always squeak
For, prithee don't you see,
We leave the oiling to be done
By Mr Nobody.

He puts damp wood upon the fire,
  That kettles cannot boil.
His are the feet that bring in mud,
  And all the carpets soil.
The papers always are mislaid,
  Who had them last but he?
There's no one tosses them about
  But Mr Nobody.

The finger-marks upon the door,
  By none of us are made.
We never leave the blinds unclosed,
  To let the curtains fade.
The ink we never spill, the boots
  That lying round you see
Are not our boots, they all belong
         To Mr Nobody.

Mrs Mason bought a basin,
Mrs Tyson said, What a nice 'un,
What did it cost? said Mrs Frost,
Half a crown, said Mrs Brown,

Did it indeed, said Mrs Reed,
It did for certain, said Mrs Burton.
Then Mrs Nix up to her tricks
Threw the basin on the bricks.

I do not like thee, Doctor Fell,
The reason why I cannot tell.
But this I know, and know full well,
I do not like thee, Doctor Fell.

Doctor Foster went to Gloucester
 In a shower of rain;
He stepped in a puddle,
Right up to his middle,
 And never went there again.

Dame Trot and her cat
  Sat down for a chat;
The Dame sat on this side
  And puss sat on that.

Puss, says the Dame,
  Can you catch a rat,
Or a mouse in the dark?
  Purr, says the cat.

I love little pussy,
  Her coat is so warm,
And if I don't hurt her
  She'll do me no harm.
So I'll not pull her tail,
  Nor drive her away,
But pussy and I
  Very gently will play.
She shall sit by my side,
  And I'll give her some food.
And pussy will love me
  Because I am good.

Oh where, oh where has my little dog gone?
  Oh where, oh where can he be?
With his ears cut short and his tail cut long,
  Oh where, oh where is he?

Bow-wow, says the dog,

Mew, mew, says the cat,

Grunt, grunt, goes the hog,

And squeak, goes the rat.

Tu-whu, says the owl,

Caw, caw, says the crow,

Quack, quack, says the duck,
And what cuckoos say you know.

cuckoo!

Ladybird, ladybird,
　Fly away home,
Your house is on fire
　And your children all gone.
All except one
　And that's little Ann
And she has crept under
　The frying pan.

A little cock sparrow sat on a green tree,
And he chirruped, he chirruped, so merry was he.
A naughty boy came with his wee bow and arrow,
Determined to shoot this little cock sparrow.
This little cock sparrow shall make me a stew,
And his giblets shall make me a little pie too.
Oh, no, said the sparrow, I won't make a stew,
So he flapped his wings, and away he flew.

Old Mother Hubbard
Went to the cupboard,
   To fetch her poor dog a bone.
But when she got there
The cupboard was bare
   And so the poor dog had none.

She went to the baker's
To buy him some bread.
But when she came back
The poor dog was dead.

She went to the undertaker's
To buy him a coffin.
But when she came back
The poor dog was laughing.

She took a clean dish
To get him some tripe.
But when she came back
He was smoking a pipe.

She went to the fishmonger's
To buy him some fish.
But when she came back
He was licking the dish.

She went to the tavern
 For white wine and red.
But when she came back
 The dog stood on his head.

She went to the fruiterer's
 To buy him some fruit.
But when she came back
 He was playing the flute.

She went to the tailor's
 To buy him a coat.
But when she came back
 He was riding a goat.

She went to the hatter's
 To buy him a hat.
But when she came back
 He was feeding the cat.

She went to the barber's
 To buy him a wig.
But when she came back
 He was dancing a jig.

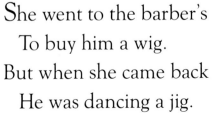

She went to the cobbler's
　To buy him some shoes.
But when she came back
　He was reading the news.

She went to the seamstress
　To buy him some linen.
But when she came back
　The dog was a-spinning.

She went to the hosier's
　To buy him some hose.
But when she came back
　He was dressed in his clothes.

The dame made a curtsey,
　The dog made a bow.
The dame said, Your servant,
　The dog said, Bow-wow.

Two legs sat upon three legs
With one leg in his lap;

In comes four legs
And runs away with one leg;

Up jumps two legs,
Catches up three legs,
Throws it after four legs,
And makes him bring back one leg.

Round and round the garden
Like a teddy bear;
One step, two step,
Tickle you under there!

Ding, dong, bell,
Pussy's in the well.
Who put her in?
Little Johnny Green.
Who pulled her out?
Little Tommy Stout.
What a naughty boy was that,
To try to drown poor pussy cat,
Who never did him any harm,
And killed the mice in his father's barn.

Two little dicky birds,
Sitting on a wall;
One named Peter,
The other named Paul.
Fly away, Peter!
Fly away, Paul!
Come back, Peter!
Come back, Paul!

Humpty Dumpty
Sat on a wall,
Humpty Dumpty
Had a great fall.

68

All the King's horses
And all the King's men
Couldn't put Humpty together again.

Oh, the grand old Duke of York,
  He had ten thousand men;
He marched them up to the top of the hill,
  And he marched them down again.
And when they were up, they were up,
  And when they were down, they were down,
And when they were only half-way up,
  They were neither up nor down.

Sing a song of sixpence,
A pocket full of rye,
Four and twenty blackbirds,
Baked in a pie.

When the pie was opened,
The birds began to sing.
Was not that a dainty dish,
To set before the king?

The king was in his counting-house,
Counting out his money.
The queen was in the parlour,
Eating bread and honey.

The maid was in the garden,
Hanging out the clothes,
When down came a blackbird
And pecked off her nose.

The Queen of Hearts
She made some tarts,
  All on a summer's day.
The Knave of Hearts
He stole those tarts,
  And took them clean away.

The King of Hearts
Called for the tarts,
  And beat the knave full sore.
The Knave of Hearts
Brought back the tarts,
  And vowed he'd steal no more.

Hickory, dickory, dock,
The mouse ran up the clock.
The clock struck one,
The mouse ran down,
Hickory, dickory, dock.

Three blind mice! Three blind mice!
See how they run! See how they run!
They all ran after the farmer's wife,
Who cut off their tails with a carving knife,
Did you ever see such a thing in your life,
As three blind mice?

Old King Cole
Was a merry old soul,
   And a merry old soul was he.
He called for his pipe,
And he called for his bowl,
   And he called for his fiddlers three.

Now every fiddler, he had a fiddle,
And a very fine fiddle had he.
   Oh, there's none so rare,
   As can compare
With King Cole and his fiddlers three.

When good King Arthur ruled this land,
   He was a goodly king.
He stole three pecks of barley meal,
   To make a bag-pudding.
A bag-pudding the king did make,
   And stuffed it well with plums.
And in it put great lumps of fat,
   As big as my two thumbs.
The king and queen did eat thereof,
   And noblemen besides.
And what they could not eat that night,
   The queen next morning fried.

One, two,
Buckle my shoe;

Three, four,
Knock at the door;

Five, six,
Pick up sticks;

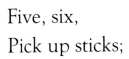

Seven, eight,
Lay them straight;

Nine, ten,
A big fat hen;

Eleven, twelve,
Dig and delve;

Thirteen, fourteen,
Maids a-courting;

Fifteen, sixteen,
Maids in the kitchen;

Seventeen, eighteen,
Maids in waiting;

Nineteen, twenty,
My plate's empty.

Simple Simon met a pieman,
    Going to the fair.
Says Simple Simon to the pieman,
    Let me taste your ware.

Says the pieman to Simple Simon,
    Show me first your penny.
Says Simple Simon to the pieman,
    Indeed I have not any.

Simple Simon went a-fishing
    For to catch a whale.
All the water he had got
    Was in his mother's pail.

Simple Simon went to look
    If plums grew on a thistle.
He pricked his finger very much,
    Which made poor Simon whistle.

Jack be nimble,
Jack be quick,
Jack jump over
The candlestick.

Jack Sprat could eat no fat,
His wife could eat no lean,
And so between the two of them,
They licked the platter clean.

Little Tommy Tucker
　Sings for his supper.
What shall we give him?
　White bread and butter.
How shall he cut it
　Without e'er a knife?
How can he marry
　Without e'er a wife?

Little Jack Horner
Sat in a corner,
　Eating a Christmas pie.
　He put in his thumb,
　And pulled out a plum,
　　And said, What a good boy am I!

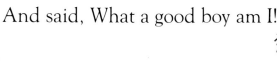

Little Boy Blue,
Come blow your horn,
The sheep's in the meadow,
The cow's in the corn.

Where is the boy
   Who looks after the sheep?
He's under a haycock
   Fast asleep.
Will you wake him?
   No, not I,
For if I do,
   He's sure to cry.

Old Mother Goose,
    When she wanted to wander,
Would ride through the air
    On a very fine gander.

Mother Goose had a house,
    'Twas built in a wood,
Where an owl at the door
    For sentinel stood.

She had a son Jack,
     A plain-looking lad,
He was not very good,
     Nor yet very bad.

She sent him to market,
     A live goose he bought.
See, mother, says he,
     I have not been for nought.

Jack's goose and her gander
     Grew very fond.
They'd both eat together,
     Or swim in the pond.

Jack found one fine morning,
     As I have been told,
His goose had laid him
     An egg of pure gold.

Jack ran to his mother
The news for to tell,
She called him a good boy,
And said it was well.

Jack sold his gold egg
To a merchant untrue,
Who cheated him out of
A half of his due.

Then Jack went a-courting
A lady so gay,
As fair as the lily,
And as sweet as the May.

The merchant and squire
    Soon came at his back,
And began to belabour
    The sides of poor Jack.

Then old Mother Goose
    That instant came in,
And turned her son Jack
    Into famed Harlequin.

She then with her wand
    Touched the lady so fine,
And turned her at once
    Into sweet Columbine.

The gold egg in the sea
    Was thrown away then,
When an odd fish brought her
    The egg back again.

The merchant then vowed
    The goose he would kill,
Resolving at once
    His pockets to fill.

Jack's mother came in,
    And caught the goose soon,
And mounting its back,
    Flew up to the moon.

This little pig went to market,

This little pig stayed at home,

This little pig had roast beef,

This little pig had none,

And this little pig cried, Wee-wee-wee,
     All the way home.

Tinker   Tailor   Soldier   Sailor

Thumbee,
Wizbee,
Long man,
Cherry tree,
Little Jack-a-dandy.

One, two, three, four, five,
Once I caught a fish alive,
Six, seven, eight, nine, ten,
Then I let it go again.
Why did you let it go?
Because it bit my finger so.
Which finger did it bite?
The little finger on the right.

Rich man   Poor man   Beggar man   Thief

Wee Willie Winkie runs through the town,
Upstairs and downstairs in his nightgown,
Rapping at the windows, crying through the lock,
Are the children in their beds?
For now it's eight o'clock.

See, saw, Margery Daw,
    Johnny shall have a new master;
He shall have but a penny a day,
    Because he can't work any faster.

Goosey, goosey gander,
Who stands yonder?
Little Betty Baker.
Take her up and shake her.

Goosey, goosey gander,
  Whither shall I wander?
Upstairs and downstairs
  And in my lady's chamber.
There I met an old man
  Who would not say his prayers,
I took him by the left leg
  And threw him down the stairs.

Five little pussy cats,
   Invited out to tea,
Cried, Mother, let us go.
   Oh do! For good we'll surely be.
We'll wear our bibs and hold our things
   As you have shown us how—
Spoons in right paws, cups in left—
   And make a pretty bow.
We'll always say, Yes, if you please,
   And, Only half of that.
Then go, my darling children,
   Said the happy Mother Cat.
The five little pussy cats
   Went out that night to tea,
Their heads were smooth and glossy,
   Their tails were swinging free.

They held their things as they had learned,
  And tried to be polite.
With snowy bibs beneath their chins
  They were a pretty sight.
But, alas for manners beautiful,
  And coats as soft as silk!
The moment that the little kits
  Were asked to take some milk,
They dropped their spoons, forgot to bow,
  And — oh, what do you think?
They put their noses in the cups
  And all began to drink!
Yes, every naughty little kit
  Set up a miaou for more,
Then knocked the tea-cups over,
  And scampered through the door.

Two brothers we are,
  Great burdens we bear,
    On which we are bitterly pressed.
  The truth is to say,
  We are full all the day,
    And empty when we go to rest.

Diddle, diddle, dumpling, my son John,
  Went to bed with his trousers on.
One shoe off, and one shoe on,
  Diddle, diddle, dumpling, my son John.

To bed! To bed!
Says Sleepy-head.
Tarry awhile, says Slow.
Put on the pan,
Says Greedy Nan,
We'll sup before we go.

Matthew, Mark, Luke and John,
Bless the bed that I lie on.
Four corners to my bed,
Four angels round my head.
One to watch and one to pray
And two to bear my soul away.

Bye, baby bunting,
Daddy's gone a-hunting,
Gone to get a rabbit skin
To wrap the baby bunting in.

Rock-a-bye, baby,
　Thy cradle is green,
Father's a nobleman,
　Mother's a queen.
And Betty's a lady,
　And wears a gold ring.
And Johnny's a drummer,
　And drums for the king.

Hush, little baby, don't say a word,
Papa's going to buy you a mocking bird.

If the mocking bird won't sing,
Papa's going to buy you a diamond ring.
If the diamond ring turns to brass,
Papa's going to buy you a looking-glass.
If the looking-glass gets broke,
Papa's going to buy you a billy-goat.
If that billy-goat runs away,
Papa's going to buy you another today.

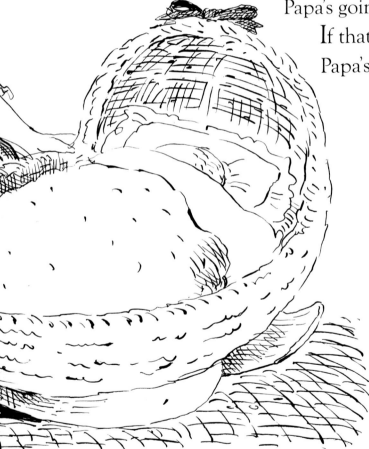

Hush-a-bye, baby, on the tree top,
When the wind blows the cradle will rock.
When the bough breaks the cradle will fall,
Down will come baby, cradle, and all.

I saw a ship a-sailing,
A-sailing on the sea,
And oh, but it was laden
With pretty things for thee!

There were comfits in the cabin,
And apples in the hold.
The sails were made of silk,
And the masts were all of gold.

The four and twenty sailors,
That stood between the decks,
Were four and twenty white mice
With chains about their necks.

The captain was a duck
With a packet on his back,
And when the ship
Began to move
The captain said,
Quack! Quack!

Who killed Cock Robin?
I, said the Sparrow,
With my bow and arrow,
I killed Cock Robin.

Who saw him die?
I, said the Fly,
With my little eye,
I saw him die.

Who caught his blood?
I, said the Fish,
With my little dish,
I caught his blood.

Who'll make his shroud?
I, said the Beetle,
With my thread and needle,
I'll make the shroud.

Who'll dig his grave?
I, said the Owl,
With my pick and shovel,
I'll dig his grave.

Who'll be the parson?
  I, said the Rook,
  With my little book,
I'll be the parson.

Who'll be the clerk?
  I, said the Lark,
  If it's not in the dark,
I'll be the clerk.

Who'll carry the link?
  I, said the Linnet,
  I'll fetch it in a minute,
I'll carry the link.

Who'll be chief mourner?
  I, said the Dove,
  I mourn for my love,
I'll be chief mourner.

Who'll carry the coffin?
  I, said the Kite,
  If it's not through the night,
I'll carry the coffin.

Who'll bear the pall?
  We, said the Wren,
    Both the cock and the hen,
We'll bear the pall.

Who'll sing a psalm?
  I, said the Thrush,
    As she sat on a bush,
I'll sing a psalm.

Who'll toll the bell?
  I, said the Bull,
    Because I can pull,
I'll toll the bell.

All the birds in the air
Fell a-sighing and a-sobbing,
When they heard the bell toll
For poor Cock Robin.

NOTICE
To all it concerns,
This notice apprises,
The sparrow's for trial
At next bird assizes.

It's raining, it's pouring,
The old man is snoring.
He bumped his head
On the back of the bed
And couldn't get up in the morning.

Rain, rain, go away,
Come again another day.

Christmas is coming,
The geese are getting fat,
Please to put a penny
In the old man's hat.
If you haven't got a penny,
A ha'penny will do;
If you haven't got a ha'penny,
Then God bless you!

One for sorrow, two for joy,
Three for a girl, four for a boy,
Five for silver, six for gold,
Seven for a secret ne'er to be told.

Lavender's blue, dilly, dilly,
  Lavender's green;
When I am king, dilly, dilly,
  You shall be queen.
Call up your men, dilly, dilly,
  Set them to work,
Some to the plough, dilly, dilly,
  Some to the cart.
Some to make hay, dilly, dilly,
  Some to cut corn,
While you and I, dilly, dilly,
  Keep ourselves warm.

The lion and the unicorn
    Were fighting for the crown;
The lion beat the unicorn
    All around the town.

Some gave them white bread,
    And some gave them brown;
Some gave them plum cake
    And drummed them out of town.

This is the house   that Jack built.

This is the malt   that lay in the house that Jack built.

This is the rat,   that ate the malt
that lay in the   house that Jack built.

This is the cat,   that chased the rat, that ate the malt
that lay in the   house that Jack built.

This is the dog,  that worried the cat, that chased the rat,
that ate the malt   that lay in the house that Jack built.

This is the cow  with the crumpled horn, that
tossed the dog, that worried the cat, that chased
the rat, that ate the malt that lay in the house that Jack built.

This is the maiden all forlorn, that milked the
cow with the crumpled horn, that tossed the dog,
that worried the cat, that chased the rat, that ate the malt
that lay in the house that Jack built.

This is the man all tattered and torn, that kissed the
maiden all forlorn, that milked the cow with the crumpled
horn, that tossed the dog, that worried the cat, that chased the
rat, that ate the malt that lay in the house that Jack built.

This is the priest all shaven and shorn, that married the
man all tattered and torn, that kissed the maiden
all forlorn, that milked the cow with the crumpled horn,
that tossed the dog, that worried the cat, that chased the rat,
that ate the malt that lay in the house that Jack built.

This is the cock that crowed in the morn,

that waked the priest all shaven and shorn,

that married the man all tattered and torn, that kissed the

maiden all forlorn, that milked the cow with the crumpled horn,

that tossed the dog, that worried the cat, that chased the rat,

that ate the malt that lay in the house that Jack built.

This is the farmer sowing his corn, that kept

the cock that crowed in the morn,

that waked the priest all shaven and shorn, that married the

man all tattered and torn, that kissed the maiden all forlorn,

that milked the cow with the crumpled horn, that tossed the dog,

that worried the cat, that chased the rat, that ate the malt

that lay in the house that Jack built.

This is the horse and the hound and the horn,

that belonged to the farmer sowing his corn,

that kept the cock that crowed in the morn,

that waked the priest all shaven and shorn,

that married the man all tattered and torn,

that kissed the maiden all forlorn,

that milked the cow with the crumpled horn,

that tossed the dog,

that worried the cat,

that chased the rat,

that ate the malt

that lay in the house that Jack built.

If all the seas were one sea,
What a *great* sea that would be!
If all the trees were one tree,
What a *great* tree that would be!
And if all the axes were one axe,
What a *great* axe that would be!
And if all the men were one man,
What a *great* man that would be!
And if the *great* man took the *great* axe,
And cut down the *great* tree,
And let it fall into the *great* sea,
What a splish-splash that would be!

I saw a peacock with a fiery tail
I saw a blazing comet drop down hail
I saw a cloud with ivy curled around
I saw a sturdy oak creep on the ground
I saw an ant swallow up a whale
I saw a raging sea brim full of ale
I saw a Venice glass sixteen foot deep
I saw a well full of men's tears that weep
I saw their eyes all in a flame of fire
I saw a house high as the moon and higher
I saw the sun at twelve o'clock at night
I saw the man who saw this wondrous sight.

Here we go round the mulberry bush,
The mulberry bush, the mulberry bush,
Here we go round the mulberry bush,
On a cold and frosty morning.

This is the way we wash our hands,
Wash our hands, wash our hands,
This is the way we wash our hands,
On a cold and frosty morning.

This is the way we wash our clothes,
Wash our clothes, wash our clothes,
This is the way we wash our clothes,
On a cold and frosty morning.

This is the way we go to school,
Go to school, go to school,
This is the way we go to school,
On a cold and frosty morning.

This is the way we come out of school,
Come out of school, come out of school,
This is the way we come out of school,
On a cold and frosty morning.

Index of First Lines

118